Supermum

Mick Manning and Brita Granström

W

FRANKLIN WATTS

NEW YORK • LONDON • SYDNEY

Supermum is everywhere!
Swinging, swooping, swimming, scooting.

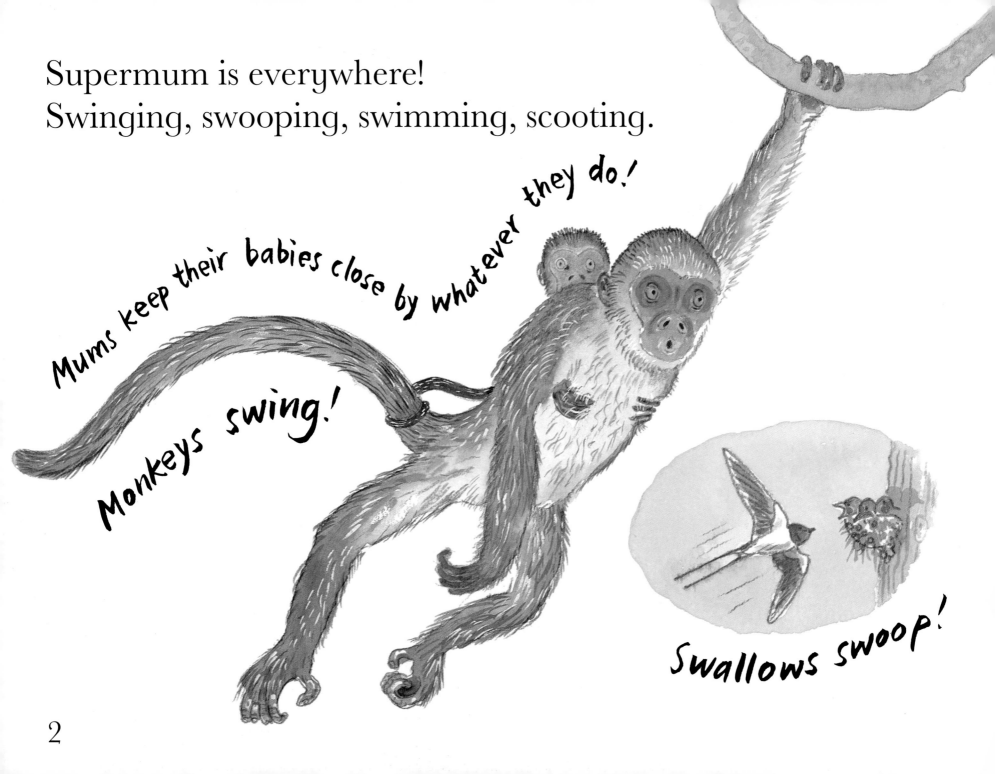

Mums keep their babies close by whatever they do!

Monkeys swing!

Swallows swoop!

2

Supermum comes in all shapes
and sizes, with lots of legs,
lots of fur, a tail, or even scales!

Mouthbrooders shelter their
babies in their mouth!

4

We call the person we grow inside 'mum'. We can call the grown up who looks after us 'mum' too.

Wildebeeste mums have horns.

Shieldbugs make good mums.

5

Supermum has babies!
She lays eggs – or she carries
her babies inside her body
until they're born.

Some snake mums guard their eggs...

We all need a mum or we couldn't be born.
Mums bring new life into the world.

Blue whales are the biggest mums on earth!

Cats can have lots of babies.

Human mums carry their babies inside their tummy for nine months.

7

Supermum knows the best games —
hide and seek, tickle, king of the castle
and lots of others.

Stoat mums get up to
all sorts of tricks!

Many babies, from wolf cubs to you,
learn by playing with their mum.

Supermum talks to her babies –
in lots of different ways!

11

Supermum will do anything for her little ones!
She'll go out in a storm to get her baby food.

Penguins walk for days to find fish for their babies.
Your mum goes out in all weathers for your food too!

Supermum is brave! If you threaten her babies, she'll scratch! She'll fight! She'll bark! She'll bite!

From swans to insects, many mums will fight to protect their babies.

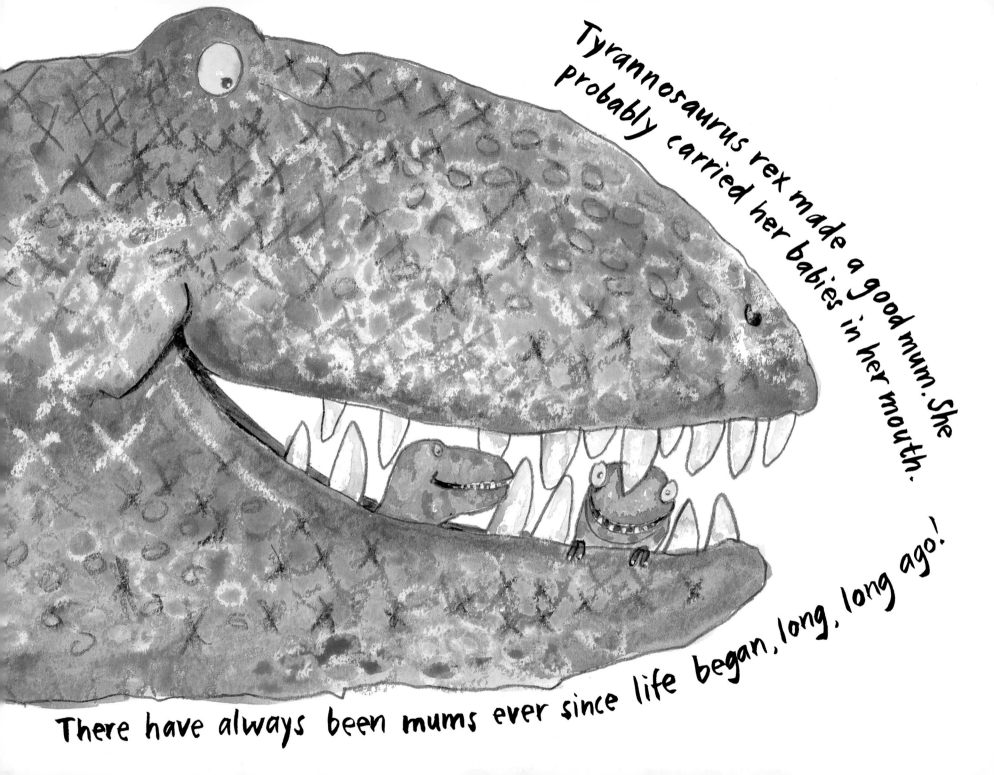

Tyrannosaurus rex made a good mum. She probably carried her babies in her mouth.

There have always been mums ever since life began, long, long, long ago!

Supermum is gentle!
She might look scary, but she always treats
her own babies **very** carefully.

Mums are very gentle
with their own children.

Supermum knows best!
She knows just what her baby likes to eat.
Worms, beetles or biscuits?
Supermum even knows your favourites.

Different baby animals like different baby foods — and mums know best!

Waspgrubs eat caterpillars. Osprey chicks eat fish...
What do you like best?

19

Supermum gives the best wash and brush up! She keeps her babies clean and tidy.

Babies need to be clean. Stale food is a breeding ground for germs!

20

Supermum is a nest-builder, a burrower,
a cave-dweller – a home-maker!
She tucks her babies in all sorts of cosy places.

A chimney pot!

A bird's nest!

A hole in the ground!

Even a crack in a wall ... or a little wooden bed!

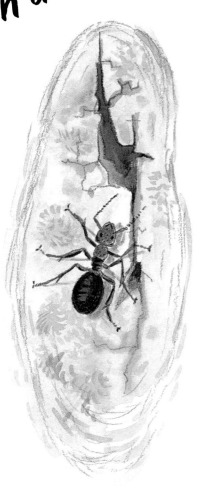

Supermum is a cuddle expert!
She'll nurse her babies to sleep, holding them
close while they have the happiest dreams.

cuddling is a good way for mum and baby to show how much they love each other.

25

Supermum is wide awake!
Even on the darkest night, she's always
ready to feed her hungry babies.

owl mums hunt mice
in the dark...

Human babies can wake up anytime for a feed!

27

Supermum has always been different shapes and sizes…

and she always will be.

mums are supermums!

29

Supermum Index

Ant – See page 23. An ant's nest is started by a queen ant. She lays all the eggs that hatch into the thousands of ants that will live there.

Barn owl – See page 26. Barn owl mums hunt for rats and mice to feed to their babies.

Blue whale – See page 6. Blue whale mums have a baby every two or three years.

Brown bear – See page 5. Brown bear mums look after their cubs for over three years.

Cat – See page 7. Cat mums can have a 'litter' of kittens once a year.

Dolphin – See pages 10 and 11. Dolphin mums look after their babies for about a year and a half.

Lynx – See page 25. Lynx mums have between one and five kittens at a time.

Monkey – See page 2. Monkeys carry their babies on their back or around their tummy.

Mouse – See page 22. Mouse mums can nest under floorboards or even in old birds' nests.

Mouth brooder –See page 4. These fish protect their babies inside their mouths.

Orca – See page 3. (Sometimes called killer whales.) Orca mums teach their babies to hunt.

Ostrich – See pages 10 and 11. Ostrich mums lay about 15 eggs at one time.

Penguin – See page 12. Emperor penguins nest in huge colonies a long walk from the sea.

Polar bear – See pages 10 and 11. Polar bears usually have two cubs at a time.

Rabbit – See page 22. Rabbit mums have lots of babies – up to 84 every year!

Raccoon – See page 22. Raccoon mums often bring up their babies in towns and cities.

Shield bug – See page 5. Shield bugs chase away other insects who try to eat their young.

Snake – See page 6. Not all snake mums guard their eggs. Some just lay them and leave them.

Stoat – See page 8. Stoat mums are fierce if their babies are in danger.

Swallow – See page 2. Swallow mums feed their babies squashed-up insects.

Swan – See page 14. Mute swans will attack if you go near their nest. One wing beat could break an arm.

Tiger – See page 20. Tiger mums look after their cubs for two to three years.

Tyrannosaurus rex – See page 16. Tyrannosaurus rex was the largest meat-eating mum that ever existed on land.

Wasp – See page 19. A digger wasp mum digs a small tunnel, lays an egg and leaves a caterpillar for her baby to eat when it hatches.

Wild boar – See pages 10 and 11. (Sometimes called wild pigs.) Wild boar mums have up to ten babies at a time.

Wildebeeste – See page 5. A wildebeeste mum has one baby a year. She always keeps an eye out for danger from lions or hyenas.

Wolf – See page 8. Wolf mums have between three and seven cubs each year.

For our mums – and mums everywhere

What about superdad?

This edition 2014

First published by Franklin Watts,
338 Euston Road, London NW1 3BH

Franklin Watts Australia,
Level 17 / 207 Kent Street, Sydney NSW 2000

Text and illustrations © 1999 Mick Manning and Brita Granström
Notes and activities © 2004, 2014 Franklin Watts

The illustrations in this book were made by Brita and Mick.
Find out more about Mick and Brita at www.mickandbrita.com

Series editor: Rachel Cooke
Art Director: Robert Walster

A CIP catalogue record is available from the British Library.
Dewey Classification 519.56

Printed in China

ISBN 978 1 4451 2885 6

Franklin Watts is a division of Hachette Children's Books,
an Hachette UK company. www.hachette.co.uk